SHARING CULTURE
KAKADU

Written by STANLEY BREEDEN   Photographs by BELINDA WRIGHT

Steve Parish
PUBLISHING

CONTENTS

Left: **Jonathan Nadji** at a paperbark swamp in his ancestral lands.

KAKADU – THE LAND

In the wilds of the top end of Australia's Northern Territory is a place of towering cliffs, deep mysterious gorges, woodlands and wide open spaces where rivers meander through grasslands.

Lagoons and marshes are scattered across a coastal plain. Stone country, forests and wetlands teem with tropical life. This place is Kakadu, traditional Aboriginal land, a National Park and World Heritage Area.

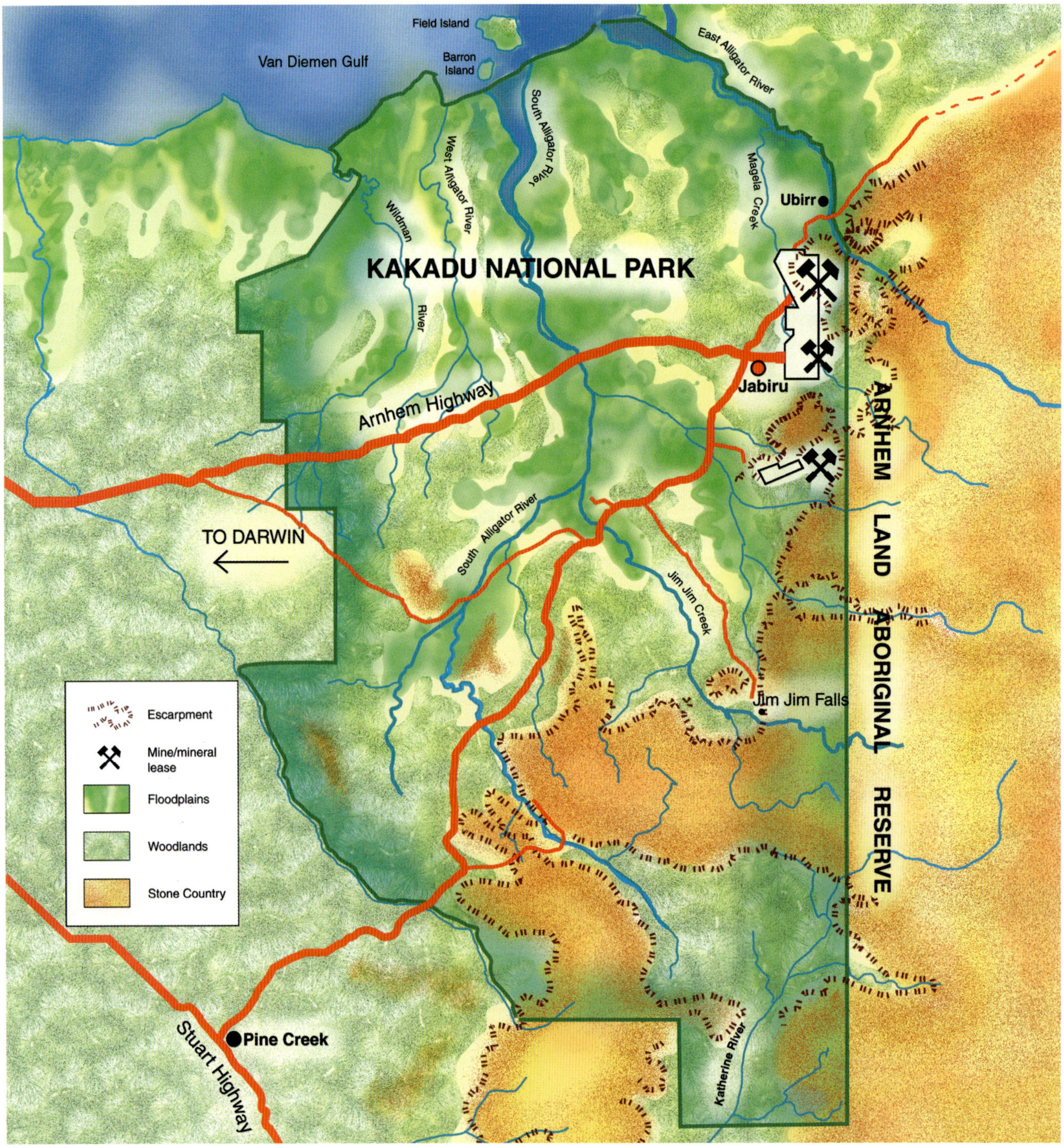

Field Island
Van Diemen Gulf
Barron Island
East Alligator River
South Alligator River
West Alligator River
Wildman River
Magela Creek
Ubirr
KAKADU NATIONAL PARK
Jabiru
Arnhem Highway
TO DARWIN
South Alligator River
Jim Jim Creek
Jim Jim Falls
ARNHEM LAND ABORIGINAL RESERVE
Escarpment
Mine/mineral lease
Floodplains
Woodlands
Stone Country
Pine Creek
Stuart Highway
Katherine River

Page 5: The cliffs of the Arnhem Land Escarpment descend 200 m into eucalypt woodlands.

Page 6: A cleft eroded in the escarpment is so narrow that the sun shines down it for only about an hour a day.

Page 7: Woodland of eucalypts and pandanus.

Above: A bend in the East Alligator River. The river is bordered by a ribbon of rainforest where it crosses the floodplain.

The Alligator Rivers flow out of Kakadu's rocky escarpments, across wide plains. The plains, grasslands, billabongs and paperbark swamps turn into great expanses of marshland during wet season floods.

These wetlands are among the most productive natural regions in the world.

The fish, waterbirds, aquatic reptiles and plants are a rich source of food for Kakadu's traditional owners, the Gagudju people.

Above: In some places the wet-season marshlands border the escarpment. Paperbark trees stand among water lily flowers.

For tens of thousands of years Aboriginal people have lived in Kakadu.

They belong to clans called Bunitj, Mirarr, Badmardi, Murumburr, Rol and many others. The extended families that make up the clans are related through marriage and united through ceremonies that maintain the people's connection with the land and with nature.

They speak several languages. The language of the Bunitj people and their neighbours is Gagudju.

Above: **Nipper Kapirigi in his country.**

In 1979 the clans of the Alligator Rivers region joined together and formed an Association to deal with the pressures of hundreds of thousands of visitors and uranium mining on their lands. They chose the name Gagudju Association, and they call themselves Gagudju.

Kakadu is a misspelling of that name.

Above: **Big Bill Neidjie (on the right) and his son Jonathan overlook their traditional lands.**

Left: Growing up in Kakadu.

Above: A Gagudju family playing cat's cradle.

The Gagudju have a deep understanding of the cycle of the seasons. They recognise six. Without the need for calendars, the Gagudju know the seasons and the foods they bring. For example, the song of a certain grasshopper signals that special yams are ready to eat.

YEGGE (MAY AND JUNE)

During *Yegge* south-easterly winds bring in the long dry season. It becomes cooler. Mornings can be misty, especially on the plains.

Many seed-eating birds such as finches and cockatoos move south to find food.

Top Left: **Long-tailed Finch.**

Bottom left: **Masked Finch at its nest.**

Top right: **Flowers of the Bridal Tree.**

Bottom right: **Flowers of a Cocky Apple or Billygoat Plum.**

Kites, birds of prey, appear in greater numbers. They are drawn to the grasshoppers and other animal life flushed from cover by fire. The Gagudju light fires on the grasslands and in the forests to clear dead grass and encourage new growth that attracts the animals they hunt for food.

WURRGENG (JUNE AND JULY)

Wurrgeng is the coolest season. Nights can be cold, especially in the heart of the stone country. Many trees are in flower, giving nectar for the sugarbag (native bees), sugar gliders, lorikeets and honeyeaters. Drying winds continue and fires are lit more often.

Above: A Sugar Glider licking nectar from the flowers of a Darwin Woollybutt. This small marsupial is an important pollinator of eucalypts.

Pages 16 and 17: During August and September Magpie Geese gather in hundreds of thousands to eat the Spike Rush tubers in drying marshes.

GURRUNG
(AUGUST AND SEPTEMBER)

The south-easterlies are ever hotter and drier during *Gurrung*. Pandanus fruit turn orange as they ripen and are ready to be gathered.

Hundreds of thousands of Magpie Geese feed on Spike Rush tubers in the drying marshes. They use their hooked beaks to dig the tubers from the mud.

The Gagudju will light the season's last fires. Later, the weather will be too hot and too dry – fire would be too intense and would destroy, not cleanse, the land.

Above: A Yellow-spotted Goanna, or Monitor, feasts on a dead barramundi.

GUNUMELENG (OCTOBER TO DECEMBER)

Heat and humidity become stifling in *Gunumeleng*. Winds can blow from any direction. Frequent and spectacular thunderstorms bring brief but heavy falls of rain. Grass begins to grow.

According to the Gagudju, the lightning is brought by *Namarrkun*, the lightning man. He lives above the clouds and carries the lightning across his shoulders. He has axes made of stone tied to his elbows and knees. He uses the axes to split the storm clouds and make the thunder.

Left: *Namarrkun*, the Lightning Man.

Top right: Kakadu and its surrounding areas experience some of the world's most intense thunderstorms.

Bottom right: Leichhardt's Grasshopper. According to Gagudju legend it is *Aldjurr*, a child of *Namarrkun*.

The people say that, during the creation time, *Namarrkun* travelled all over Gagudju country. He left some of his powerful spirit in different parts of the land – one of his eyes was embedded at the very edge of a rock plateau where it watches for the approach of the wet season from the north-west.

Soon after the first storms, large blue and orange grasshoppers appear in hidden corners of the stone country. These are *Aldjurr*, *Namarrkun's* children.

GUDJEWG (JANUARY TO MARCH)

Gudjewg is the season of rain and renewal. It begins with north-westerly winds that

Above: **Monsoonal rain tumbles down in a eucalypt forest.**

bring low monsoon clouds.

Days and days of heavy rain follow, filling the marshes and lagoons. Lush new grasses provide fresh food for the kangaroos and wallabies.

Sometimes floodwaters roar down the escarpment in waterfalls and cover the plains. In traditional times, the Gagudju took shelter in caves and beneath rock overhangs.

To non-Aborigines, *Gudjewg* is the wet season. It comes as moist monsoon winds blowing over the sea are sucked in by the heat of inland Australia.

All aquatic life – insects, frogs, turtles, crocodiles, waterbirds – take immediate advantage of the good rain to raise a new generation.

Above: **Dahl's Aquatic Frog.**

Top right: **A male Red Tree-frog's vocal sac is inflated like a balloon. His song has attracted a female.**

Left: Jim Jim Falls after heavy rain.

Above: Wet season skies over Ubirr where the stone country and the floodplain meet.

BENGGERDENG (APRIL)

Benggerdeng arrives when the wind shifts back to the east. After a few late storms, little or no rain will fall until the end of *Gunumeleng*.

Above: A female Antilopine Wallaroo in natural pasture after monsoon rain.

Left: An Intermediate Egret on its nest.

BUSH FOODS

Few places in the world are as rich in natural food as Kakadu. Edible fruits grow on trees and shrubs. Nutritious yams and other roots can be dug from the earth. Rivers, lagoons and marshes are full of fish, turtles and crocodiles. Waterbirds, especially geese, are plentiful. Kangaroos, wallaroos, wallabies, goannas and giant snakes can be hunted in the forests and the stone country. Sugarbag, wild honey, is there in plenty in hollow trees…

Even in the dry season, the Gagudju people need only spend a few hours of each day to hunt and gather their food.

Above left: People eat the stems, roots and seeds of the Pink Lotus.

Left: Nipper Kapirigi with Freshwater Crocodile eggs that he has just dug up. Crocodile eggs are a prized bush food.

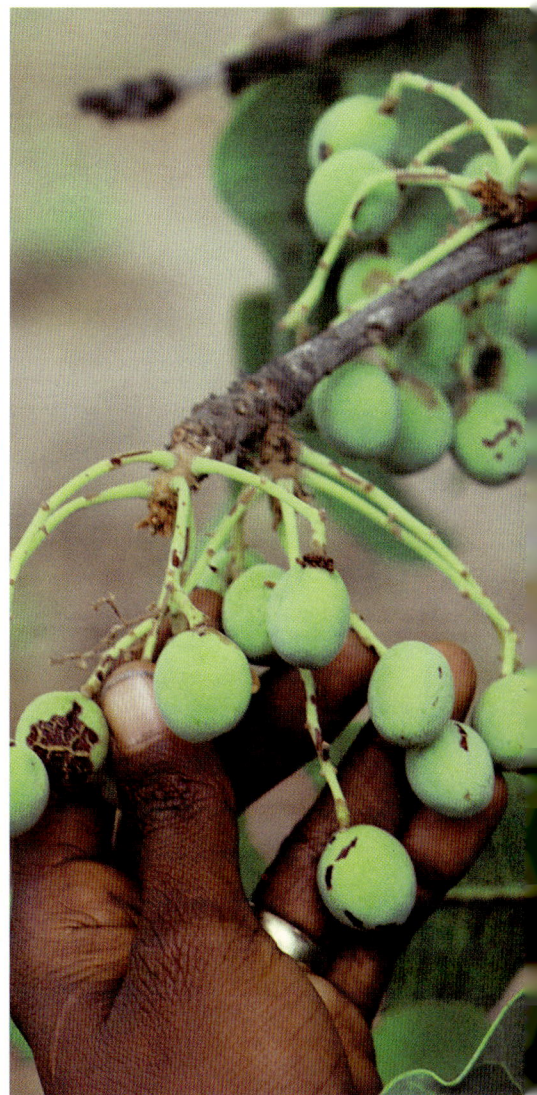

Above right: Many fruits like these Green Plums are harvested in the eucalypt forests. (Photo: Ian Morris)

Traditionally the Gagudju people used no firearms and no motor vehicles. They relied on their wits, their strength and agility, and their skill with spears, clubs and throwing sticks to catch the animals that they needed. They never went hungry.

The people's knowledge of the bush and the animals' habits told them where the flying foxes were, when the snakes were fat, when goose and duck eggs could be harvested, how to stalk wallabies....

Left: A Black Flying-fox and her young.

Top: A Wandering Whistling-Duck.

Bottom: An Olive Python.

Gagudju children start learning how to gather food when they are very young. Families often go out into the bush and everyone, young and old, will catch small animals: turtles, lizards, echidnas and bandicoots. Women and children gather most of the vegetable foods, such as fruits and tubers.

The men go out, alone or in small groups, to hunt the larger animals: big goannas, wallabies and wallaroos. Usually it is also the men who fish with spears, but everyone has a go with line and hook. When evening falls, the families get together to cook and eat the day's catch.

Above: A Yellow-spotted Goanna, or Monitor.

Right: A Gagudju boy and his catch – a Northern Snake-necked Turtle.

Pages 32 and 33: Nipper Kapirigi looks down on *Djuwarr* Creek in the stone country. By the end of the Dry during early *Gunumeleng*, the streams have stopped flowing, but the deep gorges hold chains of permanent clear pools.

Nipper Kapirigi, a man of the Badmardi clan, was the custodian of a part of the stone country called *Djuwarr*.

It is an out-of-the-way ravine where the birds and mammals found only in the escarpment can readily be seen.

During the wet season and for a short time after it, the rock gardens of *Djuwarr* overflow with brilliant flowers.

Above: **Short-eared Rock-wallaby.**

Top: Dryander's Grevillea.

Bottom: **A species of** *Mitrasacme*. During the wet season, masses of flowers carpet the ground.

THE WILDLIFE

Each kind of animal Kapirigi met had a special meaning for him and his people. The Great Bowerbird, who uses bleached bones and shells to decorate the display bower he builds, is *Djuwe*. He is a dangerous and mysterious bird who will steal your bones.

Many species of plants and animals are found only in this region's sandstone country. They are called endemic species.

For example, each major group of insects has at least one representative here that is found nowhere else. There are sandstone grasshoppers, dragonflies, beetles, flies,

Above left: Nipper Kapirigi examines the bones and snail shells that a Great Bowerbird has placed around his bower.

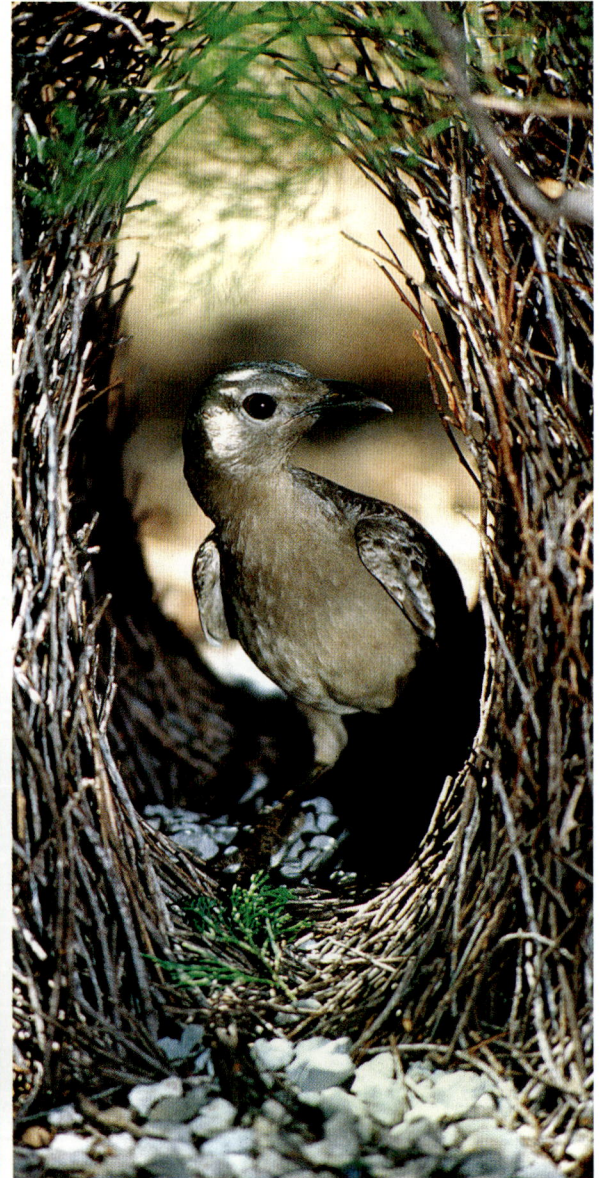

Above right: A male Great Bowerbird inside the "avenue" style bower that these birds build. He will display at his bower to attract females.

mosquitoes, termites, ants and so on. The Leichhardt's Grasshopper pictured on page 19, one of the most spectacular insects found in Kakadu, is one of these endemic species.

As many as twenty species of frogs and reptiles are endemic to the sandstone.

Above left: Rock Ringtail Possum, a sandstone endemic.

Top right: A Sandstone Antechinus eating a grasshopper.

Bottom right: The Chestnut-quilled Rock-Pigeon is found only in the stone country.

PAINTING ON ROCK

Throughout Kapirigi's country there are huge galleries of exquisite paintings, mostly of animals.

They are drawn on the escarpment's rocks. The red ochre used to paint the pictures bonds with the quartzite rocks and is almost indestructible.

Some paintings are estimated to be tens of thousands of years old. The Gagudju do not relate to the older paintings. They say these were put there by spirits at the time of the creator beings.

But the most recent paintings, including those in the X-ray style, are of great significance to the Gagudju. They link the spiritual and natural worlds.

Above: A gallery of rock paintings at *Djuwarr*. The snake is *Nawarran*, the Giant Rock Python.

Animals that are important totems and foods were painted. Many of the paintings are of animals that are honoured in ceremonies. Together, paintings and ceremonies represent to the Gagudju the life essence of the various species – kangaroo, barramundi, python, crocodile, echidna and all the others.

To stay in touch with this life force, to make sure that food remains plentiful, the custodians of the country must paint and repaint the animals. The images must not be allowed to fade.

Nowadays few, if any, new paintings are done on rock, but the art of painting on bark still lives on.

Top: Nipper Kapirigi.   Bottom: Ancient rock paintings of wallaroos.

Top: *Djawok*, the koel, a bird that is a mythological figure for the Gagudju.

Above left: Close-up of a barramundi showing the fine detail and artistry.

Above right: Echidnas.

Pages 42 and 43: Part of the *Yuwenjgayay* frieze of paintings – one of the world's great works of art.

One of the last great bark painters was Bluey Ilkirr. With his wife Susan Aladjingu he lived in the forests and woodlands. All that he needed to paint his masterpieces, Ilkirr found in the bush around him. His "canvas" was a sheet of bark he cut from a stringybark tree. His brushes were strips of bark or twigs frayed at one end. For very fine work he stripped a grass stem down to just one or two fibres. His paints – white, red ochre, yellow ochre and black – were from clays and rocks found in Kakadu.

Left: Susan Aladjingu holds a young Agile Wallaby that she reared. Beside her is a basket that she wove out of split pandanus fronds.

Above left and centre: Bluey Ilkirr cuts and removes a piece of bark from a Darwin Stringybark tree. He used it to make a large painting.

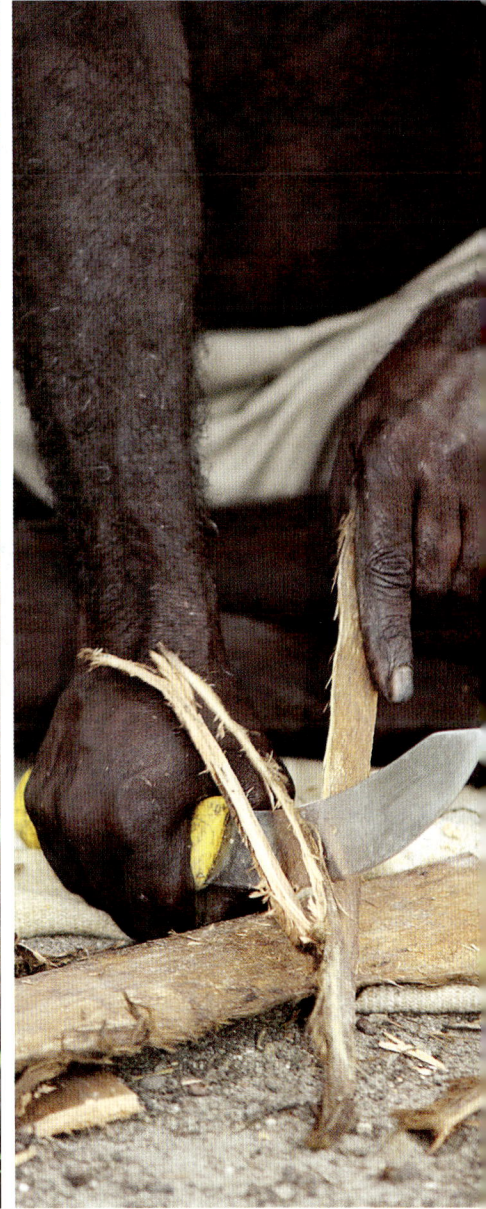

Above right: Cutting a broad brush out of tree bark.

In the pictures on these pages, Ilkirr painted animals of the East Alligator River area – wallaby, crocodile, echidna and barramundi. He called it "East Alligator *Djang*", or "East Alligator Dreaming".

Ilkirr, like the rock artists for generations before him, performed a sacred, spiritual act when he painted, an act that connected him to nature.

Above left and centre: **The animals are first painted in white.**

Above right: **The fine detail is painted in with a brush made out of a grass stem.**

Right: Ilkirr finishing his painting, "East Alligator *Djang*".

EUCALYPT WOODLANDS

More than half of Kakadu is covered by forest and woodland dominated by eucalypts.

Woodlands cover the largest area of all Kakadu's habitats. They grow on the poorer soil. The trees are low, usually no higher than 13 m, and widely spaced. Most lose their leaves in the dry season.

The forests have taller trees that grow closer together, and need deeper, more fertile soil with year-round ground moisture. As a result, the trees are evergreen. Together, the woodland and forest support more plant species than all the rest of Kakadu. Most of the Gagudju's food plants grow here.

Above: A Sugar Glider curled up in its daytime nest in a tree hollow.

Above left: At dusk the Sugar Glider emerges from its hollow to feed on flower nectar and insects.

Top right: An opening Swamp Bloodwood bud.

Bottom right: Flowers of the Darwin Woollybutt.

There are more animals on the floodplains than anywhere else, but they belong to comparatively few species. The stone country harbours the most endemic species. However, the forest and woodland are home to the greatest variety of wildlife, many of them occurring right across tropical Australia.

This diversity is not always apparent, especially during the dry season when the animals gather around small waterholes and springs.

The woodland and forest may not be as spectacular as the escarpment or the vast flocks of waterbirds on the wetlands, but their ecology is the most fascinating.

Left: Eucalypt and paperbark forest during the wet season.

Above, top: An Azure Kingfisher brings a fish to its young.

Above, bottom: A Merten's Water Goanna, or Monitor, hunting a tadpole.

Beyond the forests are the floodplains, a mosaic of grassy flats, shallow marshes and deep billabongs.

The eastern part of the plain is in Bunitj country, the ancestral home of Jonathan Nadji. Fish, including the much prized barramundi, abound in the waters. It is also the home of *Ginga*, the Saltwater or Estuarine Crocodile, and several kinds of water snake.

Weeping Paperbark trees thrive in the damp ground. They provide Jonathan with a place from which to spear fish.

Pages 54 and 55: Jonathan Nadji spearing a barramundi at *Djarrdjarr* Billabong.

Left: The East Alligator River meanders over the floodplain.

Above: A Saltwater Crocodile catches a barramundi.

The trees also support the nests of many kinds of birds, including *Marrawuti*, the White-bellied Sea-Eagle.

To the Gagudju, this powerful bird is the boss of the floodplain. He is the one who carries away the spirits of those who die.

Marrawuti made one of Kakadu's landforms – a flat, grassy area on the edge of the floodplain.

Below *Marrawuti*'s nest lives a great variety of waterbirds, large and small: birds, birds, birds everywhere.

Above: **A pair of White-bellied Sea-Eagles built a nest in the tall paperbark tree in the foreground.**

Right: **A White-bellied Sea-Eagle eating a barramundi.**

Every niche is filled with birds. Giant Black-necked Storks pace the shallows in pursuit of fish and water snakes. Tiny dotterels dash along muddy shores snapping up insects. Ducks and geese up-end or dive for submerged water plants.

Lotusbirds trot across floating water lily leaves, picking off small snails as they go. Terns hover, then dive after tiny fish.

Above this bustling mass of waterbirds, kites and eagles circle, ready to pounce on the unwary or the injured.

Left: A male lotusbird on his nest.

Above left: A darter calls while drying its wings.

Top right: A male Green Pygmy-goose.

Bottom right: A Magpie Goose.

The Gagudju tell many stories about the land and the animals. Each short story on its own could be compared to a legend. But when all the stories are told in their proper order and setting, they reveal the truth about all life and how to live it.

The complete story is called the Dreamtime in English.

The Gagudju say that, in the time of the creative spirit ancestors, animals could be people and people, animals. All were one.

Gurri, the Blue-tongued Lizard, travelled through the land to give to the people the rules about their relationships to one

Above: *Gurri*, the Blue-tongued Lizard.

another, and to explain how these should be followed. During his travels *Gurri* slipped and fell on his face, bruising his tongue. That is how it became blue.

In the beginning, *Gowarrang*, the echidna, was a woman, and *Almangeyi*, the Northern Snake-necked Turtle, a man.

They decided to go hunting together. They found a large snail, a delicacy. Soon they quarrelled about who should eat it. The man became so annoyed that he threw his bundle of spears at the woman. They stuck in her back and remain there to this day as quills.

Above left: A bark painting of *Gowarrang*, the echidna, eating termites.

Top right: *Gowarrang*, the echidna.

Bottom right: *Almangeyi*, the Northern Snake-necked Turtle.

To pay him back, *Gowarrang* threw a big flat stone at the man, which he still carries as his shell.

Ginga, the Saltwater Crocodile, was also once a man. One day while he slept in some dry grass near a billabong, a fire raced towards him and he accidentally caught fire. He ran into the billabong and turned himself into a crocodile. But even now his back is covered in blister-like lumps and bumps. After he had become a crocodile, *Ginga* forced a passage through the rocks to reach the East Alligator River.

Gundaman, the Frilled Lizard, is another who was once a sleek, smooth man. During an important ceremony he let his attention wander and he performed the wrong rituals, sang the wrong songs. He had not listened to the elders and they punished him. They made *Gundaman* into a rough-scaled lizard with funny looking skinny arms and legs, and loose skin around his neck.

Above left: *Ginga*, the Saltwater Crocodile, basking on a bank.

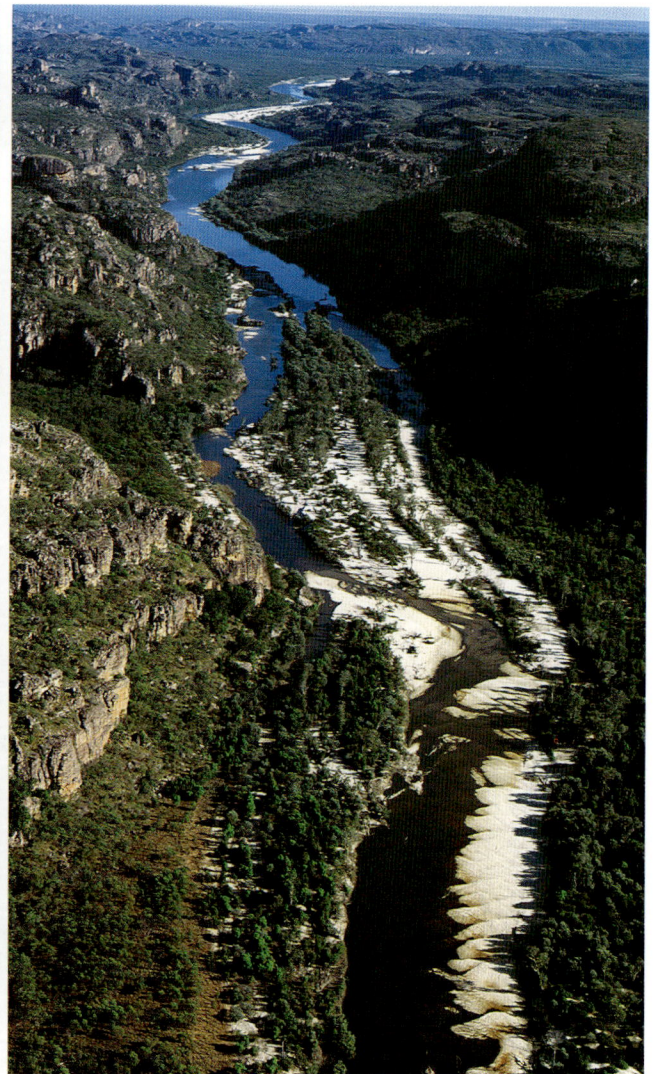

Above right: *Ginga* pushed through these rocks to reach the East Alligator River.

Above: *Gundaman*, the Frilled Lizard, did not listen to the elders.

Part of the story about *Garndagitj*, the Antilopine Wallaroo, tells that he moved around the country, digging out hollows and piling up rock outcrops.

Nearly every animal and every major place has a story.

Left: Two young male *Garndagitj*, Antilopine Wallaroos, wrestling.

Above: Nipper Kapirigi inspects paintings of *Garndagitj* – the ancestral wallaroo.

Kakadu is a thrilling place to grow up. In pools where no crocodiles live, the children swim and play for hours and hours, especially during the long, hot, dry season.

In their games they sometimes imitate Ginga, the crocodile, by hiding under the water weeds as he does, and scaring their friends. The children run and chase each other through grassy fields. Or they may run off into the bush on their own to play games and find adventure.

They learn all kinds of games like cat's cradle from their families.

Above: Susan Aladjingu, right, plays cat's cradle with her friends and family. The figure she has made represents a river turtle.

Top: Children swim and play in waterholes free of
Saltwater Crocodiles.

Bottom: A Saltwater Crocodile uses the cover of water
plants to lie in ambush in a billabong.

Some days, often in the late afternoon, the children learn something exciting that will be important to them for the rest of their lives. They may be painted in age-old tribal designs and learn traditional songs and dances. The music and dance could be just for fun, or part of an important ceremony that they must learn if they are to become proper Gagudju men and women.

But much of the day is spent having fun. Like children everywhere, they enjoy playing games like "King of the Castle", particularly on a majestic termite mound.

Left: **Ceremonial dance.**
Above left: **Being painted and learning traditional dance.**

Above right: **Playing "King of the Castle" on a termite mound.**

The Gagudju used to make everything they needed from materials they found in their country. They made axes and sharp knives out of rocks. The women made all kinds of baskets and dilly bags from the leaves of pandanus trees, grasses and other plants. They dyed the fibres with colour extracted from plant roots. Spears, clubs, dishes, paints and brushes – everything the people used was made by them with skill and ingenuity.

All these things together are called a society's material culture.

Top: Ilkirr and Kapirigi make stone knives and scrapers out of quartzite rock.

Above: Kapirigi makes a spear.

Right: A quarry where Gagudju people used to make stone tools.

Maintaining the balance between people and the natural world is called "looking after the country" by the Gagudju. The people's duty takes many forms and is lived every day of their lives.

Part of it is to teach the sacred knowledge to each new generation. This learning is absorbed over a lifetime through the teachings and examples of the elders and in a series of ceremonies.

One such ceremony is the song cycle that honours *Indjuwanydjuwa*. Felix Iyanuk enacts it in a cavern overlooking the rock that is the embodiment of that creator being.

The rock is a focal point of the area's life force. Behind him, on the cave wall, is the painted image of *Indjuwanydjuwa*.

Above: The rock that is *Indjuwanydjuwa* seen at sunset.

Right: Felix Iyanuk sings the *Indjuwanydjuwa* song cycle from a cave overlooking the rock.

Among other things, *Indjuwanydjuwa* taught the Gagudju how, when and where to hunt certain animals. In singing this song cycle in this cavern, the elder keeps a tradition stretching back for 2500 generations or more, alive.

Some of the other ways in which the Gagudju take care of the land and the

Above: **Big Bill Neidjie makes fire and burns his country following ancient traditions.**

people's relationship with it are simply to be in the country, to hunt and gather food in it, and to burn it in strict accordance with ancient tradition.

Left: The Gagudju say that fires lit in the right season cleanse the country.

Right: Brown Falcons and Black Kites scavenge animals killed by the fire.

One day, to affirm their commitment to the Law, Bill Neidjie and his son Jonathan place their hand stencils on a rock wall. It is near a sacred place high on an outcrop overlooking their country.

That evening, Jonathan attends an important ceremonial dance on the floodplain (pages 78 and 79).

In this way the ancient Law continues through each generation of the people in the clans of the Gagudju.

Above: **Big Bill shows his son, Jonathan Nadji, a hand stencil that he made when he was a boy.**

Seasons of flood, seasons of drought, masses of flowers, untold numbers of animals, swampy green plains, rough-hewn cliffs – all interwoven with the threads of the Gagudju's Dreamtime – that is the essence of this least spoilt corner of Australia.

In Kakadu, at least, it is still possible to see, to hear, to smell and to feel Australia as it was more than 200 years ago.

Above: Jonathan Nadji makes a hand stencil.

Pages 78 and 79: A ceremonial dance on the floodplain at dusk.

GAGUDJU GLOSSARY

Aldjurr. Leichhardt's Grasshopper, which, according to Gagudju legend, is a child of *Namarrkun*.

Almangeyi. Northern Snake-necked Turtle.

Benggerdeng. The season of little or no rain (April).

Djang. Dreaming.

Djawok. Koel, a bird that is also a mythological figure for the Gagudju.

Djuwarr. A place in the stone country.

Djuwe. Great Bowerbird.

Garndagitj. Antilopine Wallaroo.

Ginga. Saltwater or Estuarine Crocodile.

Gowarrang. Echidna.

Gudjewg. The season of rain and renewal (January to March).

Gundaman. Frilled Lizard.

Gunumeleng. The season of heat and humidity (October to December).

Gurri. Blue-tongued Lizard.

Gurrung. The season following the coolest, when winds become warmer (August, September).

Marrawuti. White-bellied Sea-Eagle.

Namarrkun. Lightning man.

Nawarran. Giant Rock Python.

Wurrgeng. The coolest season (June, July).

Yegge. The cooler, dry season (May, June).

ENGLISH GLOSSARY

affirm. To state something positively either in words or actions.

aquatic. Of plants and animals, living in water.

billabong. A branch of a river or creek that forms a waterhole, usually only in the wet season.

bond. To hold together firmly.

clan. A group of people who are related or who live together in a certain area.

cleft. A space or opening.

culture. All the habits, beliefs and ways of living of a group of people; the way of life children learn.

custodian. Someone who has responsibility for and takes care of something.

cycle. Something that repeats itself at regular intervals of time.

dilly bag. A bag made from woven grass or other plant fibre.

display. Of birds, behaviour that communicates with other birds, using feathers, movement, voice, objects.

dominate. To control or tower over something.

ecology. The relationship between living things and their environment.

elder. A senior person; someone who holds knowledge of traditional language, law and skills.

embed. To fix an object firmly in something.

embodiment. The state of being given body or made real.

endemic. Found only in a certain area or habitat.

erode. Of the land, to wear away as a result of wind and, mainly, rain or running water.

escarpment. A long stretch of rocky cliffs.

eucalypt. Any tree of the genus *Eucalyptus*, commonly called a gum tree.

floodplain. Flat land that is covered with water when waterways are in flood.

gorge. A piece of land that has steep cliffs on both sides.

grasslands. Usually flat land covered with grass.

humidity. The amount of moisture in the air.

ingenuity. Cleverness at inventing things.

lagoon. A body of water like a small lake.

life force. Everything that gives meaning to people's lives; the power of a people's spiritual life.

marsh or **marshland**. Land that is low and wet; a swamp.

marsupial. A mammal whose young attaches itself to its mother's nipple, usually in a pouch or fold of skin.

meander. Of a river, to wind and bend across the land.

monsoon (*adjective* **monsoonal**). A rain-bearing wind system.

mosaic. A design made up of different shapes and colours.

mythological figure. A character from a myth, which is a traditional story that usually explains something that happens in nature.

ochre. Coloured earth in yellows, oranges and reds.

paperbark. A kind of tree with thin layers of paper-like bark.

pollinator. An animal or insect that carries pollen from one flower to another.

ravine. A narrow, steep-sided, deep valley, usually one that has been eroded by a river or creek.

scavenge. Of animals, to find dead creatures on which to feed.

song cycle. A series of songs about the same subject.

species. A single kind of animal or plant; for example, all humans are one species.

stone country. The Kakadu land that has rocky outcrops and mountain ranges.

totem. Something of the natural world, often an animal, which someone considers they are closely related to.

tradition (*adjective* **traditional**). Beliefs and customs handed down from one generation of people to the next.

tuber. A thick, fleshy, rounded plant part that grows underground; a potato is a tuber.

weeping. Of tree branches and leaves, drooping down towards the ground.

wetlands. Land that is covered with water: lagoons, marshes and billabongs.